CHAMPION
Of Alaskan Huskies

Joe Redington Sr.
Father of the Iditarod

By Katie Mangelsdorf

D1456843

books   *ts.com*

ISBN 978-1-59433-245-6
eBook ISBN 978-1-59433-246-3

Library of Congress Catalog Card Number: 2011931797

Manufactured in the United States of America.

Dedication

To Dad and Mom for instilling in me a love for learning, adventure, and books.

Foreword

Joee and Pam Redington
Raymie and Barb Redington
Tim Redington

Joe Redington Sr. was destined to live his Alaska dream, homesteading in Alaska in 1948, working with sled dogs for the U.S. Army in Rescue and Reclamation, hauling freight in the winter to his Flat Horn Lake homestead, competing in early Fur Rendezvous races, numerous mid-distance races in Alaska, the Kuskokwim 300 in Bethel, the Knik 200 in his home town, the John Beargrease Race in Minnesota, the Alpirod in Europe, participation in the Winter Olympics in Lillehammer, Norway, and his 1979 McKinley climb with a seven dog team. Besides competing in the Iditarod himself a total of 19 times, he last entered the race at 80 years of age in 1997. To realize their Iditarod dreams, Joe furnished teams to mushers from Australia, England, France, Japan, Norway, Russia, and also his home country, the United States. He started the Iditarod Challenge from Knik to Nome, an "Iditarod Adventure" for those who had an interest in long-distance mushing. Joe was like a magnet to those who had an interest in the Iditarod, whether it be as a musher, fan, or sponsor of the race. His love for sled dogs and the Iditarod emanated from him, and drew people from around the world to either watch the excitement of the start of the race or the grand finish in Nome. He always felt that as long as someone had an interest to participate in the Iditarod there would always be an Iditarod. From working with sled dogs upon his arrival in Alaska, he instilled the love of mushing in his sons, Joee, Raymie, and Tim. All three had kennels of their own and competed in the Fur Rendezvous and Open North American as well as various other sprint races. Joee's son, Joee Ray, also competed in these races. Joe and Raymie each raced in the Iditarod and still operate their kennels. The legacy continues with Raymie's sons, Ray Jr. and Ryan, both Iditarod veterans.

Joe's biggest and staunchest supporter was his wife, Vi. She was just as active with the dogs as he was, from showing dogs in their early years in Alaska to mushing her own team to and from Flat Horn Lake and racing in sprint races, as well. Vi was secretary for various clubs and organizations, Aurora Dog Mushers, which the Iditarod evolved from, Knik Chapter of Iditarod Trail Blazers and the Wasilla-Knik Historical Society. This was the basis for her interest in the restoration of the Knik Hall and Dog Musher's Museum. Joe and Vi were instrumental in seeing that the Iditarod Trail was established as a National Historic Trail in 1978. Vi was a notary public and maintained her ham radio license for their many years at Flat Horn.

Eventually Joe and Vi met Katie Mangelsdorf, who was a teacher and later taught one of their grand kids in school. From Katie and her family's love of watching and keeping track of who was doing what in sled dog races, her interest to write this book about Joe was born. This became a fourteen year project, beginning with her many talks with Joe and Vi, and later gathering pictures with Joee and Raymie. This former teacher has finished this wondrous story about a couple who followed their dream of moving to Alaska to mush dogs. We hope you enjoy this book about Joe and Vi and their love affair with sled dogs, the Iditarod, and Alaska. They had an adventurous life and Joe was truly destined to be the *Father of the Iditarod*.

Joee and Pam Redington
Raymie and Barb Redington
Tim Redington

Acknowledgements

This book has taken many years to come to fruition. Throughout those years I would read and reread a letter my husband wrote supporting my vision for Joe's book. He said, "It must be done. It can be done. It will be done." And now I can say, "Ron, it is done!" Thank you for your strong, loving, and prayerful support, and for the reading and rereading to help clarify what I wanted to say. To our three children, Mollie, Julianna, and Wylie, I have loved your little pictures and notes that are still tucked in my notebook and all your words of encouragement and support. To my brother, Dan Moore, who lent his editing expertise and knowledge. And to Pam Redington for her valuable edits on the copy proof.

Many people have helped along the way, and I am so grateful for their interest and patience to make sure everything is as accurate as I can make it. Every effort has been made to contact the individuals in this book to verify the events. Some of you I was not able to reach, but your part in Joe's life was important, so I kept you in the story. And there are many people I wanted to include, but couldn't. The majority of this story is based on my conversations with Joe and Vi, with clarifications and verifications from individuals involved.

I have so enjoyed getting to know the Redington family, Joee and Pam, Raymie and Barb, and Timmy. Your help finding the pictures Joe and Vi wanted, I am so grateful for! Thank you for your support along the way. Brian Okonek and Rob Stapleton, your verification of Joe's expedition up Mount McKinley was invaluable. Sue Henry, I am so grateful my sister, Linda Kile, introduced me to you at the Fur Rondy Melodrama. Your complete support for Joe's story gave me the kick start I needed to see this story through to completion. I would also like to thank the following individuals for taking the time to talk to me about Joe and Vi and those of you who made this book possible: Terry Adkins, Terry Aglietti, Kitty Banner, Patti Bogan, Tom Busch,

Mel Behnke, Linda Chamberlain, Joe Delia, Bill Devine, Nan Elliot, Joyce and Melissa Garrison, Doug Geeting, Glenn Hitchen, Gleo Huyck, Marthy Johnson, Tom Johnson, Don Lee, Brit Lively, Dick Mackey, Lance Mackey, Frank Murkowski, Benoni Nelson, John Norman, Dave Olsen, Art Petersen, Tom Porter, Joanne Potts, Jim Reardon, Dr. Jim Scott, Dan Seavey, Frank Smith, Jane Storey, Kathy Sullivan, Rick Swenson, Deby Trosper, Tim White, Diane Williams, and Jo Wood! And Bryce Burkhart and Nicole Hall, thank you so much for helping digitize my maps.

Preface

My parents' dream to live in Alaska brought them to this great land in 1952. They raised me, my sister, and my brother in Eagle River. Our family cross-country ski trail was along part of the original Iditarod Trail from Seward to Nome. Dad's work in communications took him to some of the same communication sites Joe Redington's Rescue and Reclamation work took him. Mom loved books and started the library in Eagle River. Both of them loved the sled dog races held every year during the Fur Rendezvous in Anchorage. Our childhood sports heroes were dog mushers such as Jimmy Huntington, Gareth Wright, George Attla, Doc Lombard, and Jimmy Malemute. Then the Iditarod Race to Nome started and we had favorites starting with Herbie Nayokpuk, Emmitt Peters, Ken Chase, and Joe Redington. The dog races got us out of the house, on our skis or walking, to watch these beautiful dogs racing through winding trails in the woods and across frozen lakes. All this eventually led to the writing of Joe Redington's biography.

In 1971 I became a teacher starting out my career teaching in the Bush in Athabascan and Eskimo villages the first years of the Iditarod Trail Sled Dog Race to Nome. I began saving newspaper clippings of the Iditarod Race in 1977. For a long time I had wanted to write an adventure/biography that would capture my sixth grade students' interest. I wanted a story that showed them how a person's experiences and how they think through those experiences determines what they accomplish in life. Joe Redington Sr. was the man I wanted to write about. Teaching took all my time, so it wasn't until I retired in 1996 that I was able to call Joe and present my idea to him. There was a long pause. I thought he probably didn't like the idea. Then he said in typical Joe fashion, "When do we start?" He was quick to add, "But I don't want any book written just about me. Vi must be a part of it, because without her, I couldn't have done what I did." I agreed and we began long, wonderful visits, and looked through hundreds of his slides. They identified what pictures they wanted in the book.

Joe was an ordinary man with a not so ordinary dream and a great love and devotion to sled dogs. He was an Alaskan pioneer who showed courage, ingenuity, determination, a willingness to help others, and a love for the richness of this great land, so typical of many of the early pioneers in Alaska. He never gave up on his dream, his vision, to bring back the sled dog to Alaska villages. He did whatever it took to achieve this and became Alaska's greatest champion of the Alaskan husky.

Some people called him the Sly Fox because he had a way with words that lured the listener right into his dreams. This quality is one big reason we have the Iditarod Trail Sled Dog Race today. The Iditarod Race was built by volunteers who caught the spirit of Joe's dream. But he was also just a man who had faults like any of the rest of us. He was as tenacious as a bulldog. Some of his friends say that once he got focused on an idea, that idea was all he could see. The result was knocking heads with folks about what should or shouldn't be done or sometimes things got put on the back burner that should have been taken care of. Despite all this, he was a man of courage. He was industrious, creative, and if he said he would do something, he did everything in his power to make sure it happened. And Joe loved dogs. He worked tirelessly to preserve the Alaskan sled dog and to prove what they could do.

It is important to note that over the years a number of ideas have taken hold that are not true. Joe wanted people to know the story behind what happened. He wanted to show through his life experience how the events of the Iditarod Race to Nome unfolded and his expedition up Mount McKinley occurred.

Everything Joe did was to promote the Alaskan husky. His life was all about dogs. His idea for the long-distance Iditarod Race stands entirely by itself. Because of the vastness of Alaska, the small Native villages that grew along natural waterways and passes, the discovery of gold in Interior Alaska and on the coast, modes of transportation were trails for dog teams in the winter and boats and trails in the summer. These ancient travel routes have been used for centuries and centuries. Events that define Alaska used these old trail systems— the trails being the only connection between villages and mining camps.

The long-distance Iditarod Trail Sled Dog Race was Joe's idea. He and friends discussed going to Iditarod for a number of years. Joe's idea expanded to a race to Nome. He and two other men came up with the route of the race keeping in mind two things: (1) to get as many villages involved as possible and (2) to have a destination people could get excited about. This was done to save the Alaskan husky and the dogsledding culture that had always been a part of Alaska's history and to preserve the old freight and mail trail from Seward to Nome—the Iditarod Trail. The 1925 Serum Run had absolutely no connection to Joe's Iditarod, except that they both used part of the same ancient trail system. The connection people read about today happened later through reporters not knowing the history of the events and supporters of the Iditarod caring more about continuing the reason for the Iditarod Race than working to correct misconceptions, although they tried.

Joe passed away before the book was completed, but Vi read and helped correct much of it before she passed on. Joe and Vi's pioneering spirit is now recorded for all readers of their story, and perhaps they will go out and have their own adventures and strive to accomplish their own dreams. Now wouldn't that be grand?

Finally, I would like to add my guidelines when I was writing this book: it was written to bless readers and injure no one; it was written with truth, kindness, grace, and dignity for man; it was written to inspire, and teach through adventure; and it was written to preserve the Alaska spirit and part of Alaska's history.

David Henry Thoreau said, "How many a man has dated a new era in his life from the reading of a book." Joe's adventure to Alaska began with a book. I feel reading is so important, and to have dreams and know that anything is possible, if you hold on to a good dream and strive to achieve that dream. Joe Redington Sr. did just that.

Quotes about Joe

Nothing stops Joe. He doesn't see anything as impossible. He is determined. He focuses on his dreams. He goes on even if he's dead tired.

Jo Wood

Joe is one of the shakers and movers that helped put Alaska on the map. He is an individualist.

Frank Smith

Joe is very honest. It's nice to know you can count on him. Joe backs up all he says with deeds. He dreams and he acts on those dreams—this keeps him busy.

Bill Devine

Joe is always gungho about dogs and dog mushing. He is a visionary, a dreamer.

TOM JOHNSON

Joe is a good asset to keeping the sport of dog mushing going. He lives, breathes, and sleeps sled dogs.

DAVE OLSON

Joe is very observant. He knows how to read people.

NAN ELLIOT

Joe was one of a kind. He had such a unique, easy way of looking at things. Joe had tremendous physical endurance and mental strength. He was completely honest.

JOHN NORMAN

Table of Contents

Every boy loves their cowboy hat and Joe was no exception.

CHAPTER I

Humble Beginning

*Success is measured not so much by the position
that one has reached in life as by the obstacles
which he has overcome while trying to succeed.*

BOOKER T. WASHINGTON

Here is the story of Joe Redington Sr., sled dog musher extraordinaire. His deeds would make him a legend of the north, a champion of the Alaskan sled dog, and he would become known around the world as the Father of the Iditarod, the "Last Great Race on Earth."

Along the old Chisholm Trail on the banks of the Cimarron River, a little north of Kingfisher, Oklahoma, a canvas tent was erected. A little boy was born to James Wesley Redington and his wife, Mary Elizabeth, on February 1, 1917. They named their first child Joseph Edward Redington. This tiny little fellow was to grow up to be a strong, honest, hard-working, adventurous, and tenacious man, much like his father. In his unique and quiet way, he would inspire young and old alike. His friends say, "You can count on Joe. If he says he will do it—by golly, he will. Joe is a man of his word."

A few years later Jim and Mary Elizabeth had a second son and named him Raymond Roy Redington. In Joe's younger days Oklahoma still had a little flavor of the wild west days and his parents were friends with some of the outlaws that roamed across Oklahoma. Perhaps that connection was why Mary Elizabeth just up and left the family when the boys were quite young. Joe never knew why and his dad never spoke of her. What was important was Jim loved his sons. The women in the town where they lived didn't think he could raise the boys properly without a mother and were determined to separate them. But Jim was just as determined to keep his family of three together. That's when he packed up his sons and left Oklahoma to look for a job in the oil fields of the Texas Panhandle. Joe was around six years old.

When that job was finished, Jim moved his family again to find more work. They moved across the country with the harvesting of crops picking cotton, harvesting wheat in Minnesota and Washington, pruning plums in Oregon, picking peaches and walnuts in California, and branding turkeys in Wyoming. Jim was a hard worker and always found work somewhere. He would see each job through to the end. He never gave in to difficulties. "He never quit," Joe said. Jim told his boys, "Always keep your word. When you shake a man's hand, you must honor that gentleman's agreement."

Joe's schooling was a bit choppy because of all the moving around they did, but that didn't stop him from learning. He attended school whenever he could.

"I didn't much like school, but I would read everythin' I could get hold of. I would rather stay in and read than go out to recess."

He read magazines, newspapers, books, anything he could get his hands on. He especially enjoyed reading true stories about people, animals, and events that had taken place. This was to be Joe's ticket to success—his love of reading and his inquisitive mind.

Jack London was one author who really struck Joe's fancy. London wrote exciting stories of life in the Far North. The adventures of the Malamute Kid mushing through the wilds of northern Alaska and Canada during the Klondike gold rush days, the books *Call of the Wild* and *White Fang*, and all the different short stories he wrote, Joe inhaled. "I liked Jack London and I read just about any story he wrote." London's books opened the door to the great wonders of the untamed North Country.

These stories, no doubt, reminded him of the newspaper articles his dad had read to him soon after his eighth birthday. At that time, the end of January in 1925, a "race against death" was occurring in Alaska. Men and their dog teams carried medicine across the frozen, bone-chillingly cold expanse of Alaska to save the people in Nome, a community on the Bering Sea coast, from a deadly diphtheria epidemic. Bit by bit Joe's imagination began to spin a web of adventure that held Joe firmly in its center. And then one day, with determination in his heart, he strode up to his dad and said, "Dad, some day I'm goin' to Alaska and I'm goin' to have a dog team." His dad gave him a smile, and nodded.

Sitting by a water pump in Oklahoma is the Redington family, Ray, Jim, and Joe. This is the family no one could separate.

In the evenings Jim would sit the boys down and become the greatest of all storytellers, weaving humor into every story. The boys' eyes would snap and twinkle as their dad's stories took shape in their imaginations. Joe loved a good story.

The summer Joe was about ten, his dad and the two boys joined up with a small band of traveling gypsies. Oh, the stories that were told around the fires each night. "We traveled all over Michigan and Wisconsin during that summer," said Joe. They traveled from town to town selling baskets, butter, and hankies. Joe learned to weave baskets. That was the boys' job. The girls in the gypsy family made the hankies. The gypsy father made a kind of "butter" that looked like butter when it was cool, but turned to water when it was put on warm biscuits. Because this wasn't real butter, they were sometimes chased out of town.

The Golden Rule—Do unto others as you would have them do unto you—was important in the Redington family. "Always be honest," his dad would say. Upon seeing the deception that was going on with these gypsies, and not wanting his boys to be a part of it, Jim decided it was time to move on to other means of earning a living.

Sometimes Jim worked for the railroad delivering freight to warehouses.

In Fairbury, Nebraska, the heart of the Oregon Trail, he was working for the Rock Island Railroad. Joe was about twelve and had an opportunity to attend school for about six weeks. Walking home from school one day, he heard little puppy sounds coming from the side of the gravel road. When he went to investigate, he found a stray farm shepherd with long brown fur hiding in a small culvert with her litter of puppies. The pull of those tiny, cuddly puppies was far too great for Joe. He had this great love for dogs that could not be stopped, so he decided he would take one of those puppies home with him. Unfortunately, he didn't judge the size of the culvert well—in fact, not well at all. Joe crawled in, grabbed a puppy, and promptly got stuck. He couldn't budge an inch, not forward, not backwards.

"I didn't have no trouble when I was goin' forward, but then when I tried to back out, I had a heck of a time." What was he to do? No one was around for miles. In fact, he said, "I was in a place where nobody woulda found me for a month."

Now Joe knew that if he got himself into a predicament like this, he was on his own to get himself out.

He had been taught and was learning, again and again, never to panic or be fearful. Be calm. Stay cool.

So Joe started giving himself a little talk.

"Okay," he said, "take a deep breath and take it easy. I got myself into this culvert, so I can get myself out."

That was a calming idea. He began to relax. Then he discovered he could stretch out his body a little bit. He took another deep breath, relaxed a little more, and shrank back to his normal size. Now he was able to slide his way backwards inch by inch and out of the culvert—one puppy in hand, of course.

Joe was one happy camper. He was no longer stuck, and nestled in his arms was the cutest little puppy he ever saw. When the day came to leave Nebraska and head south to Oklahoma, the little black shepherd was snuggled into the family's Model T Ford right next to Joe. This little pup was to be just one of the many dogs Joe would love.

That's when Jim got married a second time to Evelyn Montgomery. He bought a small farm in southeastern Oklahoma for his family. "But," Joe remarked, "my dad didn't have much luck pickin' wives." Evelyn had brothers who were outlaws. Joe remembers visiting one of her brothers who was in jail after having robbed a bank.

"I was around all these outlaws and bank robbers, but my dad took real good care of us, and Ray and me, we never got into no trouble with the law." Then Joe was quick to point out, "My daddy always walked on the right side of the law."

This marriage did not last. Jim moved out of Oklahoma again to find a better place to raise his boys.

Joe had an adventuresome and creative spirit. He was always trying something new and he was a thinker. He practiced sizing up and down any situation in which he found himself. He learned at an early age never to go blindly down the road. Look first. See what needed to be done. Ask, Can I do it? Then ask, Should I do it? He was always thinking, thinking of every possibility. He thought about his abilities and what he knew he could do and then made a decision. His dad taught him to be observant and to be resourceful, to never be afraid of what life threw his way, but learn from those experiences.

"One time we was livin' in Hannibal, Missouri. We more or less just camped there. It's right on the Mississippi River. I decided to swim across. I asked a kid that was playin' there if he was a good swimmer and he said, 'Oh yah, I do a lot of swimmin'.' 'Okay, let's swim across the Mississippi.' And we did. We swam across dodgin' boats and different things. We were two or three miles down river when we got across." Joe knew there was a bridge they could cross further down the river to get back.

During Joe's teenage years America's financial market plummeted. The Wall Street crash of 1929 took the United States into the Great Depression. Joe's dad had many jobs to make ends meet. Some were good and some were not.

Joe grinned when he thought back to those days, "We didn't have much, but we never missed a meal." And they stayed together as a family.

"One Christmas was pretty scarce, but we had oatmeal for breakfast. A little sugar but no milk," remembered Joe. "Then Christmas dinner was the same thing, but Dad added a little chocolate to it. And that was Christmas Day."

They lived in New Jersey in a large city for awhile. They had never lived in a place with so many people before and it was difficult. Joe got beat up often while going to school. Soon he figured out routes to avoid the bullies, but it was a challenge for him.

"My brother and sister and I would make up our own fun and games. I went all twelve years in a one room school house."

Vi Hoffman is about six years old.

Joe's formal education took him only as far as the sixth grade, but his desire to learn never stopped. Each time he learned something, the door opened to a new area of interest. All of America was his schoolroom now. Joe's education and his honest nature were somewhat like those of the great American and true hero, Abraham Lincoln. Joe read everything he could about Lincoln. He liked the fact that when Lincoln got an idea he would gnaw on that idea for a long time. Joe took this great President's philosophy to heart. He thought about all sorts of things from every imaginable angle. Then, when all the thinking was done and his confidence was in place, he said or did whatever needed to be done.

At one point Joe's family lived in Kintnersville, Pennsylvania, on a farm for a time. That was when the Redingtons met a cute little girl, Violet Hoffman, playing along the Delaware Canal. "We swam and ice skated on the Delaware Canal," recalled Vi. "Joe used to run along the canal for about two miles when he was a young boy. He would be walking and guiding the mules up the canal. There were only two other families in the area with kids until I was in junior high school." Her friendship with the Redingtons would last a life time.

One of Joe's responsibilities was to help put food on the table. He took his 16-gauge shotgun, and went tromping through the Pennsylvania cornfields hunting for pheasants and quail. "In Pennsylvania I had Irish setters and English setters and fox hounds," remembered Joe. In those days No Trespassing signs were just not heard of. Farmers knew their fields hid birds that were a source of food for the folks living in the area, so they allowed the boys to hunt freely. The birds Joe brought home provided a good solid meal for his family. Little was said, but Joe learned that nothing feels better than to know you are contributing something of yourself to those you love.

When Joe was about thirteen his dad bought a car in Jersey City and they drove west to California to work in the fields harvesting peaches, dates, beans, and walnuts. That work finished, they sold their car in Mexico and joined many other migrant workers riding the rails to find more work. Joe remembered seeing men with their pots of stone soup, not unlike the old folktale. They rode the rails back to Pennsylvania after the growing season.

Joe grew into a handsome young man, standing about five feet, seven inches tall. He had dark, thick hair, laughing hazel eyes, a cleft chin, and a wide, warm, lopsided smile. His slim, wiry body was built for any adventure or task that came his way. His confidence grew with each adventure and by now he knew pretty much what he could and couldn't do.

In 1934 at the age of seventeen, Joe decided it was time to live out his dream—time to head to Alaska. Joe always had a convincing way of talking to folks and he loved to talk about his dream. He persuaded a friend to go along with him on this adventure to the Far North.

They took what little money they had and headed west across the United States. They got as far as Seattle, Washington, and were almost broke. They tried to find jobs to earn the $34 passage for the boat to Skagway, but jobs were scarce. Joe's dream was temporarily put on hold. Sad, but not defeated, Joe and his friend headed back to Kintnersville, Pennsylvania, where he worked for the next several years selling farm equipment.

"I was in the military five years, four months, and thirteen days. I liked the army."

Joe enlisted in the regular army.

CHAPTER 2

World War II Impact

*Responding to challenges is one of
democracy's greatest strengths.*

NEIL ARMSTRONG

Joe loved his country and its rich history.

"I've read a lot of the Constitution and I've read a lot about the ones that wrote it up and the work they put into it. I have a lot of pride in the United States. A lot of people cuss the President. I don't," Joe stated simply. "I may not have liked one of 'em, but he was still President of the United States." Joe felt it was important to show respect for the office. He never boasted about his love for his country or his patriotic feelings; rather, he showed them through his actions.

On the other side of the Atlantic Ocean, Adolf Hitler had begun his invasion across Europe. Joe, ever the voracious reader, was following these events in Europe. France had surrendered to Germany. The United States was watching closely what was going on in Europe, not wanting to get involved, but still involved.

For Joe it was time to act. So on July 23, 1940, he enlisted in the regular army.

"I didn't wait to be drafted or anythin'. I didn't want to kill nobody, but I didn't want 'em [the Nazi Germans] overrunnin' this country."

Joe became part of the Sixth Field Artillery at Fort Hoyle, Maryland. He was then transferred to Fort Sill, Oklahoma. Then Japan bombed Pearl Harbor on December 7, 1941, bringing the United States officially into World War II.

The Army recognized Joe's skills. He had a way of talking, a way of communicating, that was unique and got the point across. He was also a skilled mechanic and a creative thinker. His new job was instructing officers about the vehicles they would be driving. "I was supposed to teach 'em enough to know about it, so they could troubleshoot a vehicle and they'd know what to do."

He also taught soldiers basic electricity. "I had to do some fast studyin'," Joe commented with a twinkle in his eye, because he knew very little about electricity. He must have been a pretty good instructor because generals would step into his classes and see what he was teaching. He even had a four-star general sit in on one of his classes.

"I had no education, so I know my English must have been terrible. But I gave 'em the results they wanted and made good students," he admitted.

Before long he learned an invaluable skill. "I learned to fly in 1943 in the army with the little liaisons 'n all." Then he laughed and said, "I was a grasshopper pilot." These little lightweight civilian planes, usually reconfigured Piper Cubs, could take off and land on a dime. The army used them for rescue and reconnaissance missions. Joe loved flying, and he was flying with expert grasshopper pilots. He learned all he could about planes. Before long he was teaching airplane mechanics.

"I was an instructor there for three years and ten months durin' the war."

Following his instructor duties, he went to Infantry and Field Artillery Jump School to become a paratrooper and was transferred to Biloxie, Mississippi. He was trained to jump from a plane in full gear. He was also the first in his team of twelve men to jump from the plane. These paratroopers learned to assemble field artillery for firing in five minutes flat. The barrel of the gun was 231 pounds and required two people to lift. Teamwork was the name of the game.

"It was quite a challenge," Joe commented later.

There was only one time when he was really scared and that was on a night training mission. The men were packing their own parachutes and the sergeant in charge kept yelling, "Put 'em together! Put 'em together!"

Joe finally said, "Hey, you don't have to jump with this thing." The sergeant got mad and made Joe do one hundred push-ups.

Meanwhile, his parachute was being packed by someone else. Joe was watching this guy out of the corner of his eye as he labored through his punishment. He really didn't want to jump with that parachute, but he did.

When he jumped out, he was ready to pull the emergency cord, but fortunately the chute opened just fine.

During his stint in the army, Joe met and married Cathy Sullivan. Ray, Joe's brother also married. He married Violet Hoffman, the little girl in Kintnersville they met back in the early 1930s.

Both brothers were sent to the Pacific theater where the United States troops were fighting. Joe was assigned to General MacArthur's Special Assault Troops. He spent most of his time in the Japanese-owned Ryukyu Islands, more than one hundred small islands that stretch between Japan and Taiwan. Tiny Ie Shima, just off the west coast of Okinawa, was his destination. Ray was sent farther south in the Pacific.

Japan had kamikaze pilots who purposely dive-bombed their planes into U.S. ships on suicide missions. Okinawa saw more that 6,000 kamikaze missions that caused many deaths and great damage. Joe encountered these deadly flying planes throughout his tour of the Pacific. "I was on a little boat called the Actacogua, a little Norwegian boat. Sometimes there'd be an air attack and we'd hit the deck or head below to get away," remembered Joe. "Then there'd be a submarine attack and everyone would head for the deck. Then about that time the siren would ring and we'd head for the bottom of the boat. And I was fifty days at sea dodging submarines and airplane attacks. It was a dangerous mission"

"Right out of Hawaii we lost one of our boats. A plane dived right into it. It was our aircraft carrier to protect the group. So we lost it right away." It was badly damaged and had to go back to Hawaii."

Then Joe added, "I finally ended up at Ie Shima."

Ernie Pyle, a popular war correspondent was killed by sniper fire on the little island of Ie Shima on April 18, 1945, not too long before Joe arrived. Joe, Cathy, Ray, and Vi always read his articles. When Joe and Ray were away fighting, their wives followed Ernie's articles very closely because Ernie was right where the fighting men were and telling their stories. His writing was powerful, simple, and often understated, but so filled with compassion and hope, and really the only news they had of their husbands. Joe saw Ernie's helmet hanging on the cross above his grave and took a picture to send home. He was learning about photography in the army and loved taking all kinds of pictures. Throughout Joe's life his camera was readily available to snap thousands of pictures.

Japan formally surrendered on September 2, 1945. Joe was sent home on the *Admiral W.S. Benson* transport. "The *Admiral Benson* had fifty-five hundred troops comin' back." Shaking his head Joe stated simply, "I was sick

"Dad had all sorts of little outfits for me," said Joee.

Joee and Joe.

before we ever left the harbor, and I was sick for the whole eleven days going over to Seattle. But going over I never got sick. I was fifty days at sea, going to all the different islands, dodging submarines, and airplane attacks, and everything like that, and never got a bit sick, but comin' home I was sick every day. I never get sick when there is action goin' on."

Joe was discharged December 6, 1945, seven months after Germany surrendered and three months after Japan surrendered.

Joe liked the army and almost reenlisted, but he had a little boy, Joee, and he needed to be home with his family. He headed back home to Kintnersville with one goal in mind—to earn enough money to take his small family to Alaska.

Joe was a great salesman. He talked to the folks in the area and found out what they needed. Most of the people were farmers. So Joe showed them just what a jeep could do. He put all his creative talent to work and turned those jeeps into just about any piece of farm machinery the farmers needed. "The only thing I couldn't do," he said with a grin, "was haul a manure spreader in a barnyard."

Two years later Joe decided it was time to leave. He and Cathy now had two boys, Joee and Raymie, and a third on the way. They were having challenges in their marriage, but they thought maybe a change would help. He quit his job selling jeeps, packed up his family and belongings, and prepared to say goodbye to Kintnersville, Pennsylvania.

Joe took Cathy and Raymie to Alabama to stay with her family until little Shelia was born. Four-year-old Joee was going to ride with Joe to Alaska. Cathy would fly to Alaska with Raymie and Shelia later.

Ray, Joe's brother, was caught up in Joe's enthusiasm to move to Alaska and wanted to go, too. Ray's wife, Vi, was not so enthusiastic. In fact, she did not want to go at all. She was very close to her family and didn't want to leave them.

"I'll stay here with Tommy, [their fifteen month old son], and take care of Joee and you two can go," she said with a very determined look.

"Nope, Joee's going with me," said Joe.

"I think I was kinda in shock," recalled Vi.

Reluctantly she packed up her family's belongings, left her family and her brand-new home, and with a determined spirit joined Ray in Joe's dream. "Mom thought it was like we were goin' to the moon," Vi said. "Nobody went to Alaska in those days."

On May 13, 1948, Joe and Joee met up with Ray, Vi, and Tommy in Chicago, and the two Redington families headed to Alaska together.

Ray, Joe, and Joee in 1948 just before they crossed into the Alaska Territory. Alaska was not a state until 1959.

CHAPTER 3

Coming to Alaska

*What lured him on was, of course, the great
adventure, the eternal longing of every truly creative
man to push on into unexplored country, to discover
something entirely new—if only about himself.*

HEINRICH HANEY HASSEY

Two new bulging, canvas-covered and very dirty jeeps pulled up to Border Trading Post, a small store and gas station on the border between Canada and Alaska. Joe and little Joee piled out of one jeep, which pulled an open trailer carrying jeep parts and all of Joe's tools. He always believed in being prepared for anything. Ray, Vi, and Tommy piled out of the other jeep, which was pulling a teardrop trailer. The dusty Redingtons stretched their legs, leaving a Dalmatian and an Old English sheepdog with her newborn puppies to watch over the vehicles.

While Joe and Ray pumped gas from a fifty-five gallon drum, Vi and the children wandered over to watch a litter of small husky pups playing and tumbling end over tea kettle in the gravel and dirt. Their furry little bodies were darting every which way. Vi's smile could not get wider. She loved dogs. She found herself enthralled with these bright-eyed, curly-tailed husky pups. The owner of the trading post saw Vi playing with the puppies and asked if they wanted one. To these gentle dog lovers there could be only one answer to that question. Yes! Thus Dodger was the beginning of the Redingtons soon to be discovered career with the Alaskan husky.

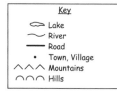
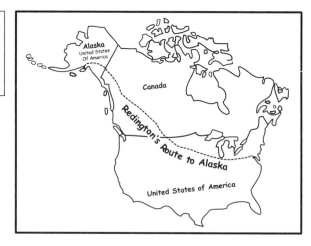